Feng Shui
of the
MIND

Amarjit Singh Modi

FENG SHUI OF THE MIND

iUniverse books may be ordered through booksellers or by contacting:

iUniverse
1663 Liberty Drive
Bloomington, IN 47403
www.iuniverse.com
1-800-Authors (1-800-288-4677)

Because of the dynamic nature of the Internet, any web addresses or links contained in this book may have changed since publication and may no longer be valid. The views expressed in this work are solely those of the author and do not necessarily reflect the views of the publisher, and the publisher hereby disclaims any responsibility for them.

Any people depicted in stock imagery provided by Thinkstock are models, and such images are being used for illustrative purposes only. Certain stock imagery © Thinkstock.

ISBN: 978-1-5320-3175-5 (sc)
ISBN: 978-1-5320-3176-2 (e)

Print information available on the last page.

iUniverse rev. date: 08/24/2017

Also By the Author

Ten Golden Rules of Living

The Heart Speaks to the Mind:
Wisdom Stories from the World's Great Masters

Mary Energy, How to Experience Joy

Christ: Mother Mary's Gift of Light

Discover Your Divine Destiny and Live with Joy

Contents

Inspired by Buddha

Introduction

In the past half century, the Universe was kind to me and allowed me to travel most of this planet. During the life journey, I met more than fifty eight thousand people from different cultures and backgrounds, religions including the bushman and aborigines of Australia.

In my conversations with them, most of them asked me how they can have joy in their life. After consulting the cosmos, I wrote a book, "Five Finger Path of Happiness," in which I shared with them if they experience true love, good health, and express the divine gifts in a loving and healthy relationship, then they can experience joy. While guiding them how to experience true joy, I discovered that love and good health are the most important elements in healthy relationships.

In my research I found that ancient Chinese wisdom was using Feng Shui to improve the relationships of outer world, which eventually will improve the relationships of inner world. "In its highest and purest form, good Feng Shui signifies perfect alignment between inner and outer worlds." —Lady Ray

During my meditation, I discovered the outer world which is the environment we live in, is influenced by the inner world of your mind and its thoughts. "Every aspect of life is anchored energetically in your living space, so clearing clutter can

completely transform your entire existence."
—Karen Kingston

This message of Feng Shui revealed to me that our mind is like a living room where reside your present, past and future thoughts, your present, past and future relationships, and your present, past and future experiences and your belief systems. And if they are not arranged properly, they can create clutter, anxiety, restlessness and lack of joy.

In this book, "Feng Shui of the Mind, "I will draw inspiration from the Chinese Feng Shui, from the wisdom of Buddha, Lao Tzu, Tolstoy, Socrates and some modern spiritual thinkers and advisors. Based on the information gathered from great masters, I will guide you how to rearrange your present, past and future relationships, present, past and future thoughts and present, past and future aspirations in the light of your gifts and life purpose.

Some of the information is based on the guidance I gave to more than fifty eight thousand of people I met and other information is drawn from the great masters from the past. By sharing my experiences with you, I hope you will experience great joy.

I hope that if you follow and practice the guidance provided by this book, you will learn how to experience true joy. If you have some of your own experiences, I will be happy if you share them with me which will be included in the future editions.

I am grateful for the Great Spirit and all of the people I met in the last half century for sharing with me their guidance, their experiences and their search for joy. I hope you will enjoy the book as much as I enjoyed writing it.

CHAPTER 1

Present, Past and Future Relationships, Thoughts, Experiences, Belief Systems

When we are young, we learn from our parents, from observation and from our experiences, and from the belief system handed over to us by our parents. In our early age, we don't question, we don't think, we just accept things that happen to us. We gather information, right or wrong, and we are unaware how people influence us, our thoughts, and sometimes we have no choice of our experiences. For example, when the relationship between our parents is not good, one of our family members is not kind and loving, and our classmates mistreat us, our teachers misunderstand us, and our parents knowingly or unknowingly pass on their experience to us.

Some of these experiences, information we gather without questioning, we carry into our adult life. When we suffer we realize that these experiences, observations, mistreatments, and unkind words from family members, classmates, friends and relatives affect us deeply, and deprive us of a happy life.

On reflection, we find that when we try to eliminate these thoughts, negative experiences, and unkind relationships, they are difficult to let go. And being young, having no experience to deal with this kind of situation, we seek the guidance of friends who are equally ignorant and dealing with their own problems. Feeling helpless, we seek therapists, counselors, and the guidance of friends. A therapist finds our problems are so deep-rooted that it will take them many years to replace the negative experiences, negative thoughts, unkind behavior and replace them with new thoughts and create a new mind.

While guiding many people of this age group, I found they require many different treatments, and a long time to let go these deep-rooted learned behaviors, painful experiences, and negative thoughts, and belief systems.

In our adult life, when we confront these experiences and we discover they are too complex to let them go, including with the help of experienced therapists, psychiatrists, and spiritual counselors. It creates great crisis in dealing with life. We cannot focus on our studies, we create crisis in our relationships, and end up getting sick. And when our attempts fail, we just give up dealing and get very confused. And this confusion creates so much restlessness, lack of peace of mind, and leads us to bad choices, like unhealthy relationships and drugs.

In my wisdom readings, I discovered that most of the counselors and therapists either took too long to deal with crisis or only gave partial solutions. And when they asked me my guidance, I consulted the old masters, like Buddha, Lao Tze and Socrates, and found unless they replace the negative belief systems, let go unhappy experiences, and replace unhealthy relationships with healthy relationships, and empty their mind of negative thoughts, and replace them with healthy and positive thoughts, they will find it difficult to have peace of mind and joy in their life.

They inspired me to create the "Feng Shui of the Mind" system to resolve the difficult experiences and life choices.

CHAPTER 2

Present Relationships Tools of Feng Shui of the Mind

Feng Shui of the Mind deals with proper rearrangement of thoughts, experiences, relationships, and our belief system. It is very similar to feng shui of a room. When in a room the furniture and objects are scattered and unorganized, it creates difficulty to work in an efficient and peaceful way. Then we throw away the old and unneeded furniture, bring some new furniture, rearrange so energy can flow freely. This inspires positive thinking, creates a peaceful environment, and increases productivity. And we keep arranging, keep replacing old and obsolete furniture, until when we walk in the room we feel inspired, free flow of energy, and peaceful environment to work.

Guided by the outer Feng Shui in our place of work, we learned that we can use the same technique by working with our mind, where the furniture is relationships, thoughts, experiences, and belief systems. We discovered that by letting go old and unhealthy relationships and negative past experiences, and replacing negative thoughts with positive thoughts, and also by replacing negative belief systems with positive belief systems, we begin to discover joy and peace in our life.

How to rearrange unhappy experiences, unhealthy thoughts, painful relationships, negative belief systems, which are comparable to non-rent paying tenants. In the first place, they give no benefit, and second they don't allow new experience to enter. We have to deal with each one of the experiences separately and with deep commitment to release them so they don't return back and make our life difficult and unhappy.

Parents

We cannot replace our parents, but we can let go of the experience they gave us. This letting go is a spiritual practice. First we forgive them. Secondly we forgive ourself that when we acquired this experience we were innocent. Third we let go of the anger and resentment we feel. Finally we light a candle and send them light and love. And we do this until we are free. It won't be short-term, we have to do it until we feel free of their influence and experiences.

By thanking our parents for all the positive experiences they gave us, our focus on negative experience will diminish. In a dark room if we shout, the darkness increases. But bring a little candle, and the darkness disappears. By focusing on the joy, love and support our parent gave us, and not focusing on the painful negative experiences, our joy will increase and pain will diminish. And when the memory of painful experience comes, you pray, and thank the universe that what you learned you don't have to learn again. And by creating new positive experiences, we let go the old and painful experiences. And continue this process until you're totally free.

Relatives and Friends

We can use the same process when we work with the negative experiences from relatives and friends and painful experiences we gathered unknowingly. And if you choose once a week, take ten minutes to live in the present moment, and at the end observe our thought processes when the mind is quiet, and list all the unhealthy belief system we acquired and negative thoughts we let in our mind with awareness. We make a list of negative experiences and negative thoughts. For example, if you doubt, create faith. If you fear, experience love. If you are unhappy, do service or volunteer work. If you don't like yourself, count the blessings of life which make you unique.

Find one of the most difficult friends or relatives who has everything negative, and try to find one good thing in them. Then instead of being a "garbage inspector", the mind will be clear and you will be only thinking positive thoughts and begin to love yourself. When you are very unhappy and can't deal with your life situation, do an act of kindness, for example, feed a cat or a dog, talk to a stranger and say thank you, help a blind man to cross the street, and do pet-sitting for a friend. And also help someone to buy groceries who is sick and cannot do that. This will change you from negative mood to positive mood and help you discover your divine nature.

Discover some of these types of activities on your own, based on your past experiences, learn from your friends what they do when they are unhappy, and discover new ways to perform simple acts of service.

CHAPTER 3

Future Relationships

By preparing the present, we take care of the future. And since we are very clear, we learned how not to be affected by negative people, negative experiences, we have learned how not to let other people affect us, and how not to accept negative experiences, and not allow other people to mistreat us. And that is what allows unhealthy thoughts to enter our mind.

And when we meet the people with negative belief systems and unhealthy experiences, we sent them light and love so their negative thoughts and experiences stay with them and we don't allow ourselves to be affected by them. What we learned in chapter 2 by practicing and adopting those techniques we can keep our mind in a healthy state, healthy environment, and free from negative thoughts.

Now our mind is trained only to accept positive thoughts, positive experiences, invite healthy relationships and adopt healthy belief systems. And when we are aware of the people we meet who try to give us negative experiences we are fully aware not to accept and let the negative experiences stay with you. Now you are in a position where they can't affect you.

Then our inner thinking from a joyful mind will affect positively all the outer experiences, attracting new people, new experiences, new relationships.

Chapter 4

How to Make Choices from the Heart

I'm the founder of the "Seven Direction School of Choices," and before you start making any new choices, first you start above which means all the new technology and new ideas yet to come. Then consult below, which means all the wise men who died before we are born by consulting their wisdom, their books, and their experiences. Then we go to four directions, which is not just north, south, east, west, but wherever information is available. And finally the seventh direction is your heart, and when you go to the heart it will guide you what information is right for you to make the right choice, and that is the ultimate and perfect guidance we can get for making new choices.

In order to get information yet to be known, we meditate, empty our mind, and whatever information comes from the sky we write it down. And then go to Google, and see all the new information they have gathered for the subject for which you are going to make decision, gather all the information known or yet to be discovered, before you go to your heart to make the decision.

If you need to know how to work with the school, you can send email and I will guide you for free how to work with seven directions and how to work with the heart.

Printed in the United States
By Bookmasters